Let's Talk About It

A Guide for Talking to Children After the Suicide of a Loved One

Written and Illustrated by
Laura Camerona, CCLS

Commissioned by:

Contributions and edits by:

Susan Dannen, LISW
Lindsey Jenkins, LISW
Kristi Kerner, CCLS

Copyright © 2022 by Words Worth Repeating, LLC

This book is intended to be read to a child by a trusted adult.

The advice and words within may not be suitable for every child or every situation. It is suggested that the reader looks through the tips before reading this book with children.

The author would like to remind readers that the involvement of a mental health professional or support group is recommended.

Book best suited for children ages 6-12.

This book was not written to address a reader's suicidal thoughts. If you or someone you are reading this book with has suidal thoughts, call a Suicide Hotline.

US National Suicide Hotline: 9-8-8

If outside of the United States, a quick internet search can find a hotline near you.

No part of this publication may be reproduced, stored in a retrieval system, or transmitted in any form or by any means, electronic, mechanical, photocopying, recording, or otherwise, without the written permission of the author. Specific requests may be sent to laura@wordsworthrepeating.com.

ISBN 978-1-7367884-9-3 Paperback

www.wordsworthrepeating.com

Suicide is a concept that general society avoids talking about. So, when we experience a suicide in our close network, even people who are very comfortable explaining hard things to kids can struggle to find the right words. Suicide can be a complex and possibly scary subject. It is important to be honest with children without overwhelming them with details.

Children are all different, and as their caregivers, you know them best. If you read through this book, and you feel like your child isn't ready for it developmentally, you can say, "Our loved one died because their brain was very sick". For young children, they may not have a complete understanding of what "dead" is. Ask your child, "What do you think dead means?" You can remind them that dead means that the person's body and brain don't work anymore. You can explain to them that the person who died can not become alive again after they are dead. There is a lot of children's literature about death. If you think a book would be helpful, check out the library or local bookstore to find one that is a good fit for your child and your beliefs about death. In addition, many communities have grief support professionals and programs for children.

For many kids, that simplistic explanation will not be enough. It is good to keep in mind that if you use the words suggested previously, there are many ways that a person's brain can be "sick". Kids can interpret a headache as being "sick" or another mental illness could be explained as a brain being "sick". If your child is processing at this level, it is likely your child is ready to hear more. Phrases in this book can help you clarify the differences. If you hear the child use the word suicide, it is likely that they are ready for this book.

As a caregiver, being honest with your child may feel uncomfortable. For a long time, there has been a stigma surrounding suicide. People often feel like they should hide it and not talk about it. This is in the heads of many adults, but it is not, yet, in the heads of children. You can help break the stigma by having open conversations about it with your child. Open honest conversations with children build trust and a foundation for appropriate grieving as a family. If others question your decision to be honest with your children, share this book with them!

In conversations about your loved one, a child may ask you a question that you are not prepared to answer. It is okay to tell them, "I'm not sure of that answer, but let me find out for you" or, "That's hard for me to talk about, let me think about the best way to explain it to you." Be sure to go back to them and answer the question when you have decided how you want to say it. If it is hard to find the words, there are many therapists and counselors that work with grieving children. Reach out to your child's school, doctor, or local funeral home to get connected to resources. A mental health professional can help support your child regarding the specifics of your family's experience. This can give your child a safe space to express feelings and help them learn to take care of their own mental health.

You are not in this alone.

Tips for Adults Sharing this Book with a Child:

-Read through the book first without children present.

-If it seems scary or too hard to share this information with a child, remember being honest and supporting them through something hard strengthens your relationship. When you are honest, they are more likely to come back to you with their questions or feelings.

-If you are trying to decide whether to share this with a child, consider the possibility that the child could hear the information from another source. Children listen to adult conversations and children talk to each other. Although it is a hard conversation, it can help a child to hear the information clearly from you, instead of piecing together rumors and bits of information from other sources.

-When you share this book with a child, try to choose a time when you won't be rushed or interrupted. Avoid reading before bedtime, as children need time to process things.

-Remember that it is okay for a child to see you being sad. If reading this book with a child triggers an emotional response, do your best to explain. For example, "I feel sad because it reminds me how much I miss _____. It is okay to be sad when you miss someone."

-If the child does not react to this book in the way you expect, that is okay. Children process things differently than adults. The child may have no questions or seem uninterested, they may ask you about it days later, or they may seem sad after the book. All of these responses are okay.

-This book does not address different ways people die by suicide, but it may come up in your conversation. Be prepared to explain in simple terms how your child's loved one died avoiding excessive details. They may ask questions about it. Answer the child's questions, but try to follow it with '_____ did it because of how their brain was very sick'. As a caregiver, you can tell them that some things will be for talking about when they are older.

-Be prepared to stop when a child has a question. Answer the child's questions with simple, but honest words. Read the book with a child at their pace. If they want to stop reading or start talking about something else, follow their lead. Try to return to it another time.

-This book was specifically created for people who have had a loved one die of suicide. It may not be appropriate for other situations.

-If you are reading this with a child, and they share that they have had suicidal thoughts, do not downplay their feelings or their statement. Suicidal thoughts should be taken seriously no matter how they are shared. If they are willing to share, ask questions to find out more. Get them connected with a mental health professional, as soon as possible.

-For anyone who is having suicidal thoughts, contact a Suicide Hotline. There are people that can help every day at any time. (United States Hotline listed on Copyright Page)

Someone I cared about died. When someone dies, it means their body and brain stop working, and they can not become alive again.

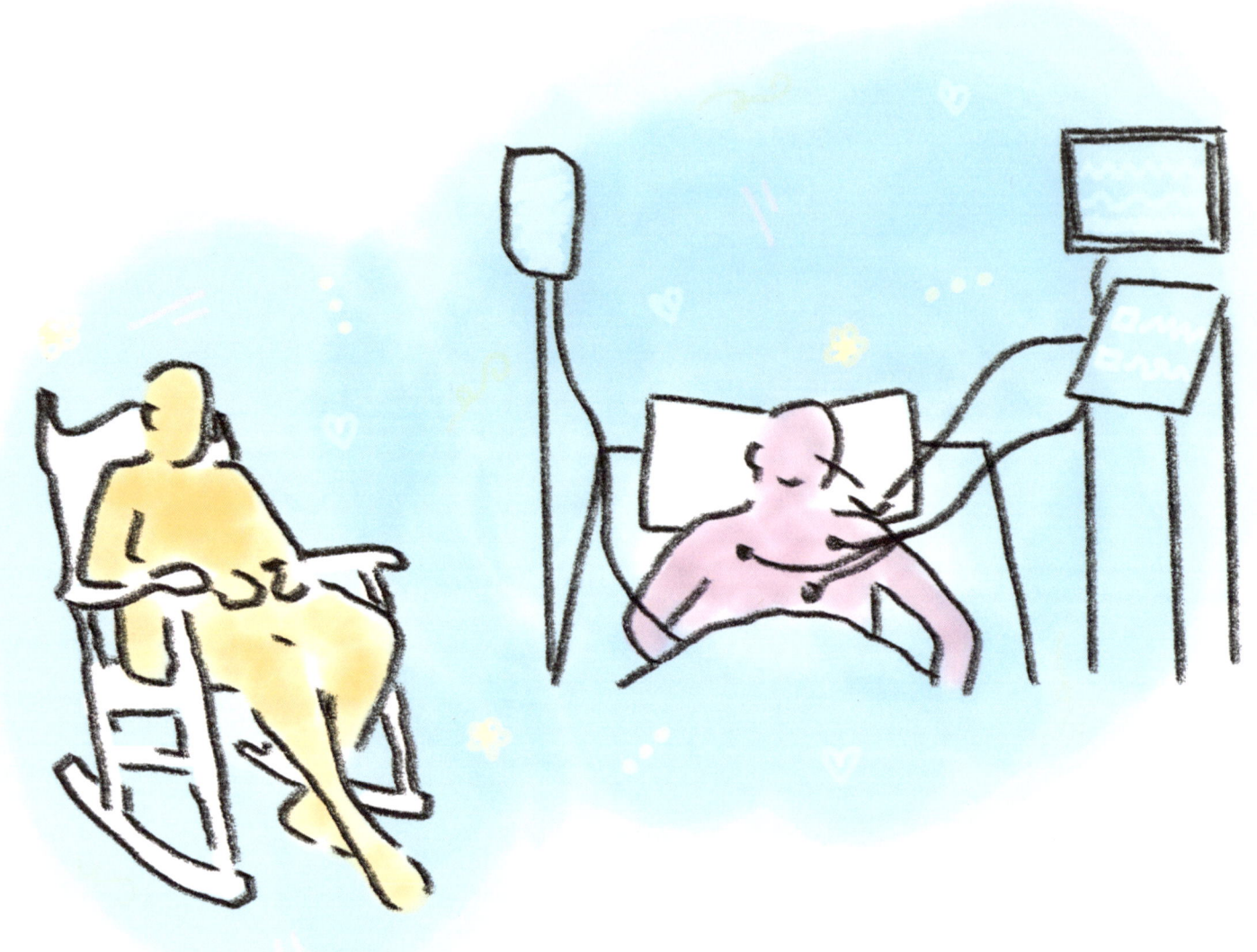

People's bodies can stop working for a lot of reasons. Some people die because their bodies get old and important parts of their bodies stop working. Some people die because a part of their bodies gets too sick or gets hurt.
My person died of suicide.

Suicide is not the same as someone dying of illllness or on accident. Suicide is when someone hurts their own body bad enough that they die, on purpose.

It's hard to understand why someone would hurt themselves. It is hard to understand why a person would try to die.

Doctors and scientists tell us that people hurt themselves and die of suicide because something isn't working right in their brains. Their brains are very sick and make them feel like it's better not be alive anymore.

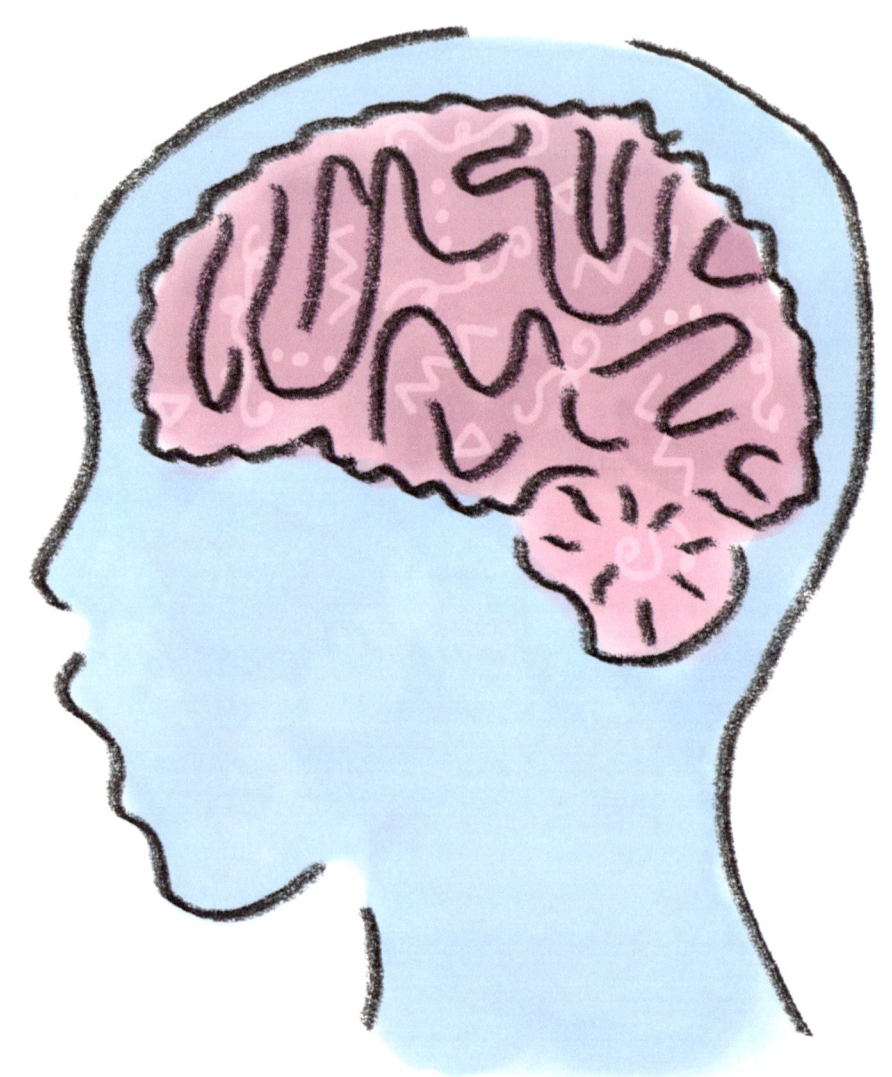

Our bodies can have many kinds of sickness, from a little cold to feeling so sick we need to go to the hospital. Our brains are like that too. Our brains can be a little sick, very sick, or somewhere in between.

There are lots of ways to heal a brain and help a person feel better. Doctors can work with each person to figure out what helps their brain. My person lost hope that they could find a way to feel better.

Hope is the feeling that the next day could be better, that things will eventually get easier. Even when life is very hard, we can always find hope. With suicide, the brain causes the person to feel like nothing will help them feel better.

When a person dies of suicide, it does not make them a bad person. It just means their brain wasn't working right. My person's brain couldn't feel hope.

When I think about suicide, I feel a lot of things. Sometimes, I feel confused, and sometimes, I feel angry. A lot of the time I feel very sad. Sometimes, I feel normal and happy. All of these feelings are okay.

Sometimes, I wonder why my person would hurt themself. I wonder if maybe they didn't love me or the people around them.

It was not because my person didn't love me. It was not because my person didn't have a good life. It's important to remember that people die by suicide because their brains aren't working right. My person died because a part of their brain was very sick and kept them from feeling hope.

My person is not the only person who has died of suicide. My family is not alone. Many families have felt the way that my family is feeling.

Many people have found that it helps to talk about it. Talking about my person and my feelings can help a lot. What I share and who I share it with is up to me. I can also tell people that I am not in the mood to talk about it.

I can decide who I want to talk to about my person and my feelings. I could choose a family member, a friend, a counselor, or maybe another person who knows someone who died of suicide.

Other people in my family are having a lot of different feelings, just like me. They might be confused, angry, or sad, too. Sometimes, they might be happy or even laugh at good memories of our person. Sometimes, we might be feeling the same thing, and sometimes, we might feel different. Our feelings don't have to match.

When I notice my family member having big feelings, it is not my job to try to fix it. I can choose to do something on my own, or I can offer to be close to them and give them hugs.
Big feelings are okay.

My family will always miss our person, but we do have each other. We will find ways to celebrate memories and be there for each other on hard days. With time, our family will find our best ways to move forward.

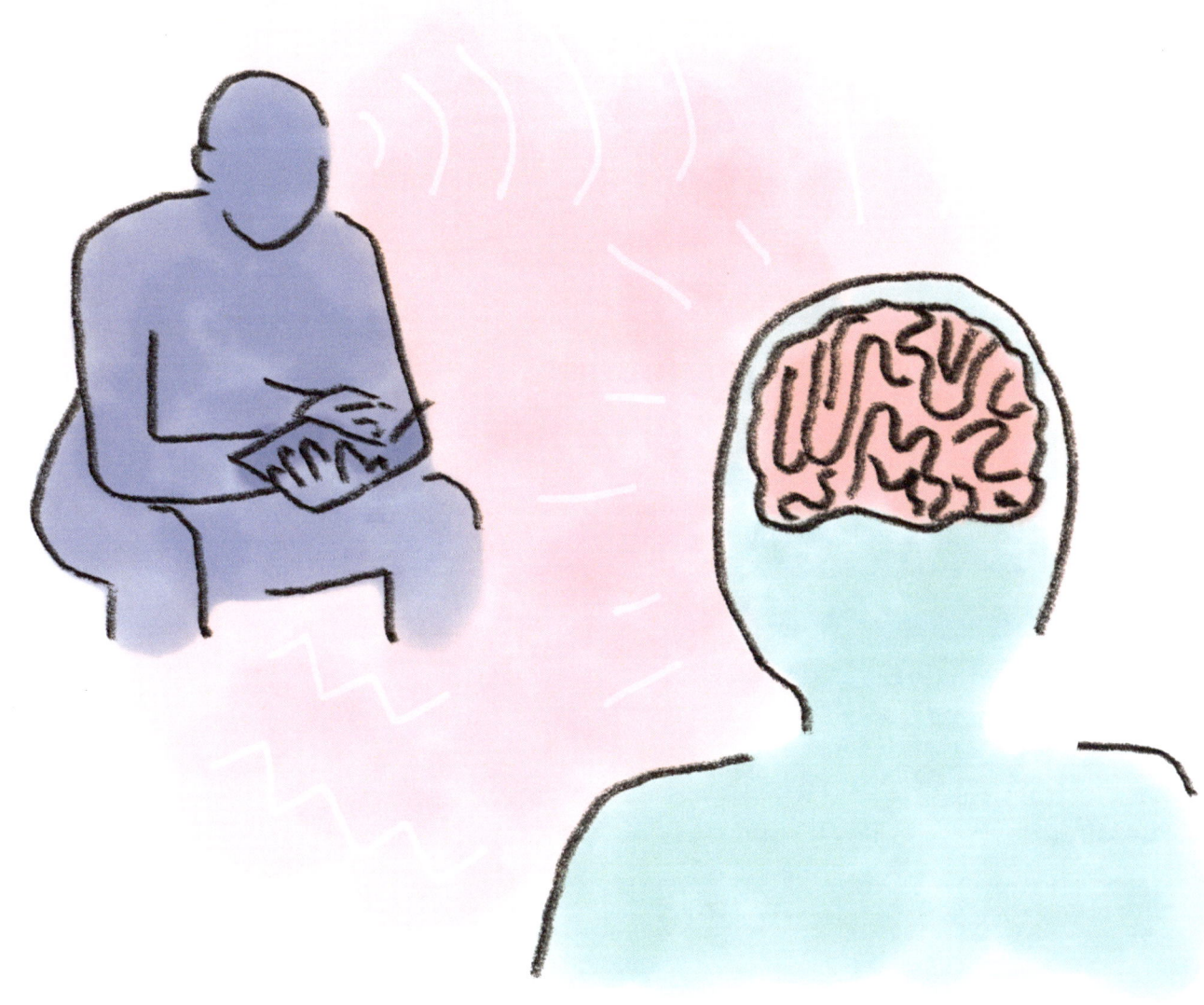

By talking about our people, we can make others aware that suicide happens because of how a person's brain is working. We can remind people that if their brains aren't working in healthy ways, there are people who can help. There are a lot of ways to heal a brain.

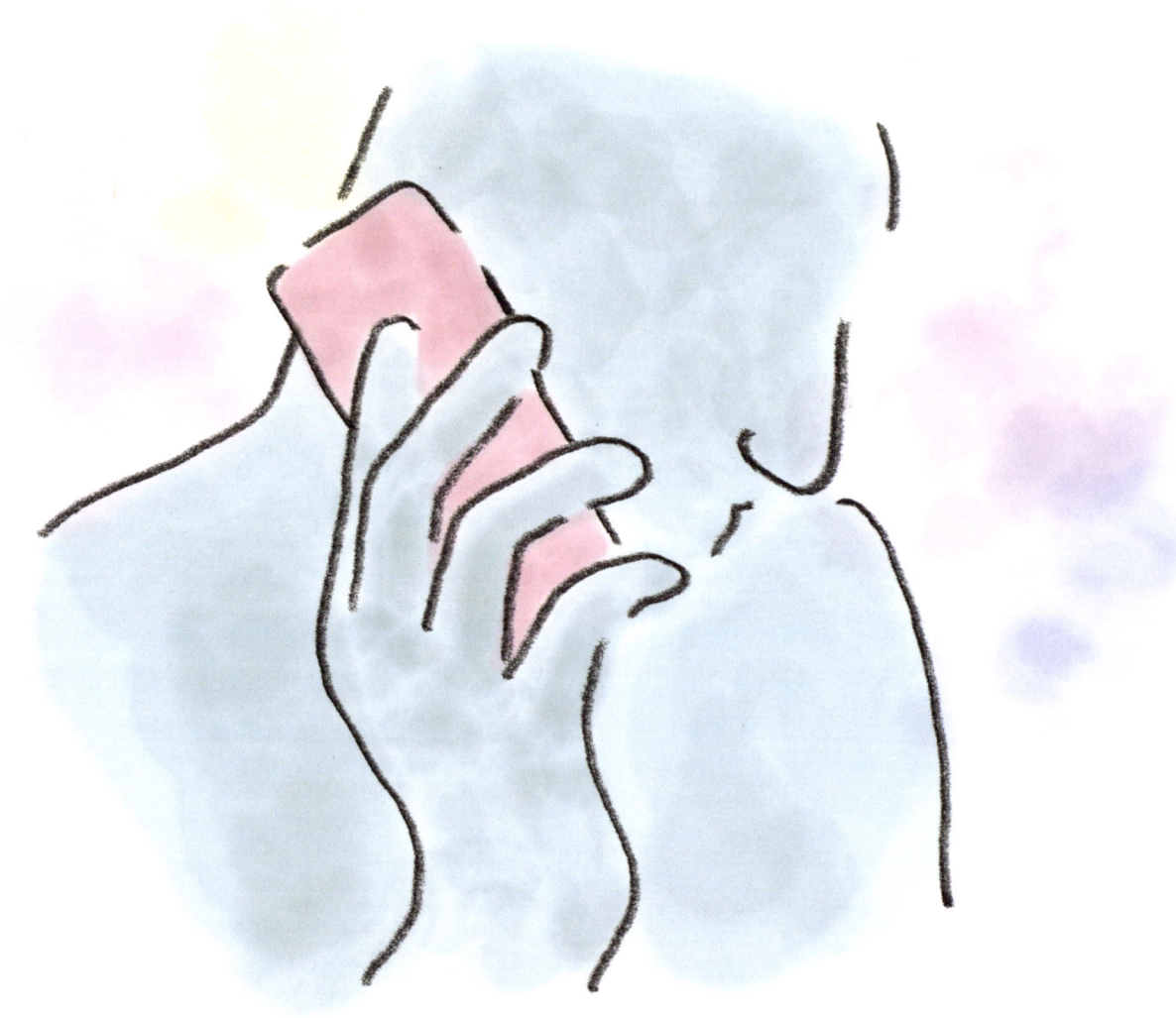

If a person is thinking about suicide, there are helpers the person can call. These helpers will talk with the person as long as they need and will help them find a doctor or a place to go for more help.

Someone who I cared about died of suicide. I miss them. I have so many feelings about it. I can talk about it. I am not alone.

What's your favorite memory of your loved one? Is there something you loved to do together?
Draw a picture or write about this memory.

When I think about my loved one, I can feel it in my body.
Draw what you feel and where you feel it in your body.

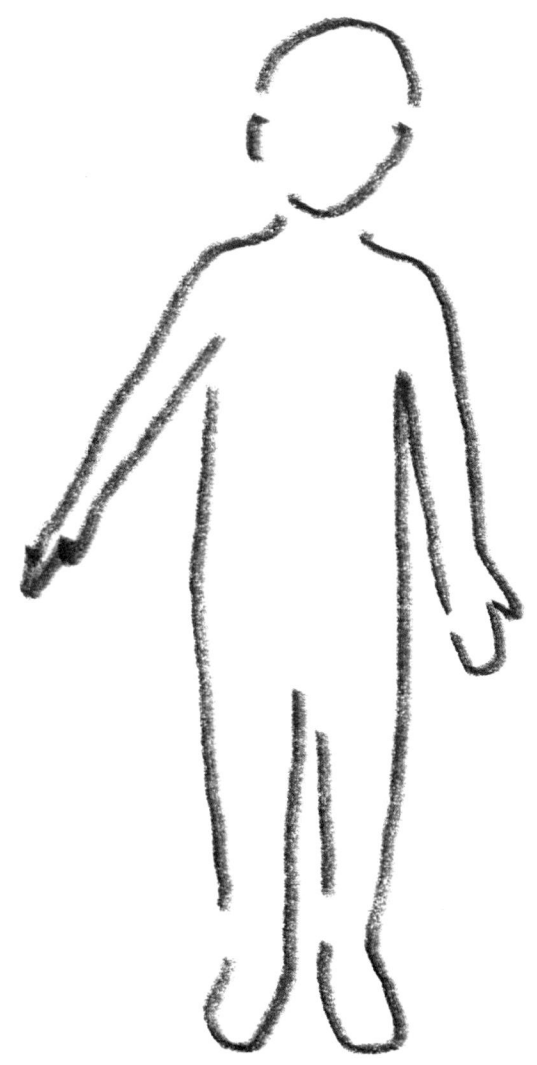

Did you include feelings like sad, angry, comfort, and happy?
Where do you feel these things in your body?

Other ideas for ways to remember your loved one:

-Write a letter to your loved one.

-Create a garden stone (kits can be found at craft stores). Put it in a place where kids can go and visit when they want to think about or talk to their loved one.

-Decorate a mason jar with pictures, jewels, glitter, or tissue paper - whatever reminds the child of their loved one.
Put a candle inside. On special days, light the candle as a family.

-Attend a walk in remembrance of your loved one. Being surrounded by people who have been through something similar can be helpful at all ages. Giving a few hours in memory of the person can also give your child a reason to get to talk about their loved one.

-Help your child make a piece of jewelry that is symbolic of your loved one. This could be beads on string, embroidery thread weaving, or paper beads with messages inside. Let the child help decide which beads/colors are symbolic to them. Wearing the jewelry can help a child feel the person with them or like they haven't been forgotten.

-Create a book about the loved one. You can find blank books or notebooks at many stores. Fill the book with drawings, stories or poems about the person, notes to the person, ... anything.

-Lastly, never hesitate to reach out to a mental health professional. If you aren't sure how to find the right person, you can talk to the child's school or doctor, and they can help you find resources in your area. Adults and kids grieve differently. A professional can help you find the best ways to support your child.

www.ingramcontent.com/pod-product-compliance
Lightning Source LLC
Chambersburg PA
CBRC100223100526
44590CB00008B/148